Text copyright © 1997 by Crane Hill Publishers
Illustrations copyright © 1997 by Sweetwater Press

Library of Congress Cataloging-in-Publication Data

The redneck night before Christmas / by E. J. Sullivan; illustrated
by Ernie Eldredge.
     p.   cm.
Based on Clement Clarke Moore's The night before Christmas.
ISBN 1-889372-00-5 (paperback)
ISBN 1-57587-069-X (hardbound)
1. Santa Claus–Poetry. 2. Christmas–Poetry. 3. Rednecks –
Poetry. I. Moore, Clement Clarke, 1779-1863. Night before
Christmas. II. Title.
PS3569.U346665R43 1996
811'.54–dc20   96-27294
                                                                          CIP

CRANE HILL
PUBLISHERS
Birmingham, AL 35222

The Redneck Night Before Christmas

Wrote Up by E.J. Sullivan
Drawed by Ernie Eldredge

It was the night before Christmas, when all through the trailer park
Not a pop-top was poppin', not even Ole Blue barked.

Our stockin's was hung over the space heater with care,
In hopes Santy would fill 'em with Viennas and beer.

The kids was asleep in their NASCAR pj's,
Dreamin' of Goo Goo Clusters, Moon Pies, and RC's.

And Earlene in her curlers
and me in my John Deere cap
Had just settled into our La-Z-Boys
for Wheel of Fortune and a nap.

Then out in the vacant lot I heard such a commotion
I thought it was neighbor Clyde,
   finally got his T'bird in motion.
I heaved out of my recliner and to the window I flew,
Busted out the screen and hollered for Blue.

The moon was shinin' down
on my old wrecked cars
So bright they was sparklin'
like rusty old stars.
And I couldn't believe my
own hardworkin' eyes
When a jacked-up Ford pickup
come flyin' through the sky!

Faster'n Ole Ironhead his possums they came
And he whooped and hollered and called 'em by name:
Git up Sooner! Hi Duke! Move yer tails Yaller and Spud!
On Blackie! On Queenie! You mind me Duchess and Bud!

To the top of the satellite dish! To the top of the shed!
Now move it! Step on it! Y'all get out the lead!

You know how, on our road, when a car goes by,
There's all this dirt flies up into the sky?
That's how this crew went straight on up to my roof
With that pickup full of toys, a real nice gun rack, and
Redneck Santa too.

Then 'fore I could pop my teeth in I heard up on the tin
The scrabbling around of them flying possums of his'n.
I yanked my head back in the trailer
     and hitched up my shorts …

Down the stove vent Redneck Santa came
   with a grunt and a snort!
He was dressed in red-and-green camo
   from his neck to his feet
And I had to give him credit—he still had
   most of his teeth.
Looked like stuff from Earlene's yard sale
   slung on his back—
There was flyswatters an' Tupperware an'
   8-tracks stickin' out of his pack.

His eyes took in our humble home:
The furniture we bought on layaway in town ...
Earlene's pride, that Elvis on velvet ...
My collections of barbed wire ...
   and license plates made by relatives.

I coulda' swore I even saw a glistening tear
When his eye fell on sweet Earlene,
   a snorin' in her chair.

He kindly favored Hank, Jr., with a big round belly
That shook when he laughed like a blob of K-Y jelly.
Yep, he was fat all right, blocked out our whole
   large-screen TV,
And I had to laugh when I saw him, 'cause he looked
   just like me!

When he winked his eye I knew fer sure he'd treat us right—
Why, he might even leave me some ammo tonight!
I stood there dreamin' of whitetail while I watched him work,
Then he stopped and, like a real man, let out a fart and a burp.

He topped off our stockin's with Moon Pies
    and bottle rockets,
Then squoze up that stove vent like Spam in your pocket.

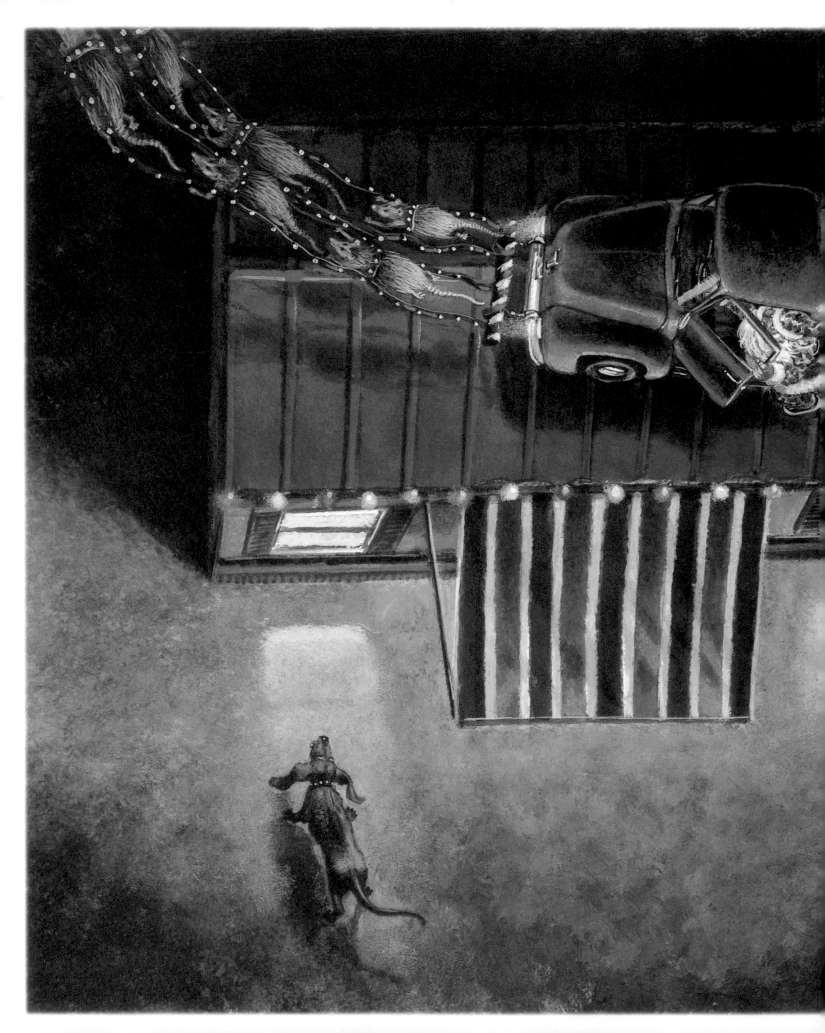

He jumped in his pickup, laid down on the horn —
  I'm not lyin'!
And they took off like white lightnin' with their
  possum tails flyin'.
But I heard him holler as he headed for the 7-11 . . .

"Merry Christmas to all, and may all rednecks go to heaven!"